Vijay Singal

ABSOLUTE ONENESS

The Journey Within

wisdom tree

First published 2011

ISBN 978-81-8328-252-9

Published by
Wisdom Tree,
4779/23, Ansari Road,
Darya Ganj, New Delhi-2
Ph.: 23247966/67/68
wisdomtreebooks@gmail.com

Printed in India at Print Perfect

Preface

Ever since the publication of my first book in the field of spiritual philosophy about a decade ago, friends and readers have been urging me to write something about the best possible way in which one can lead a contended, prosperous and progressive life.

I, for one, have always believed that there can never be a standard formula for human behaviour. There is no secret which is waiting to be revealed. Everyone, irrespective of his position in life, has to fight his own battles and search for his own truth. Still it cannot be denied that there are certain fundamental principles which almost always hold true. Accordingly, an effort has been made through this book to explore different aspects of human behaviour and examine how infallible truths and basic principles of life can be synchronised to create a blissful life.

Absolute Oneness relates to a state of being where one surrenders oneself completely to the will of the Lord and, thus, in a way, merges with Him. In the state of union, the perceived gap between the Creator and His creation, which often arises due to human ignorance, is diminished. Only when one unites comprehensively and without any expectations with the Lord, can one understand the Truth of Existence. Only then can one realise how beautiful life is, and how enjoyable the journey. The challenges one faces from time to time make it more interesting.

Absolute Oneness is in no way an essay on escapism. It, in fact, is a recipe for a simultaneous realisation of dynamic peace and harmonious growth. It prescribes how one can grow and evolve without creating complications for oneself and for others.

Inspiration for writing this book has come from varied sources. In a way, everyone with whom I have interacted in the past, at whatever level, has contributed something to it. Its contents were often discussed with H.C. Jain of the Indian Revenue Service during my posting in Mumbai. His inputs from time to time have been of immense value. Dr Sandeep Gupta, a well-known psychiatrist in Punjab, has gone through the manuscript. His endorsement and appreciation mean a lot to me. Atul Bhardwaj, as usual, has been a great support.

I am hopeful that this book will have a positive impact on the minds of its readers.

Of late,
the bond between man and Mother Nature
is weakening day by day.
The widening gap between him
and his source,
creation and its Creator,
is causing immeasurable stress
and other situations of distress.
Auto-accelerating technological developments,

and an uneven distribution of resources,
have given rise to
the comfort of a few
and the deprivation of many.
Unrealistic expectations
that are never-ending
have added to
the general sense of dissatisfaction.

Societal institutions and
moral value systems
that evolved over millennia
are either withering away,
or are trying to emerge
in forms that can be
quite horrendous.
Spontaneity seems to have vanished,

naturalness is being replaced
by a mechanical way of living,
and the fervour for life
seems to have been lost.

To regain the zing of life,
man would have to
rediscover himself
and connect with his roots.
He will have to understand
the real meaning
and make an effort
to realise
the ultimate purpose
of life.

In the quest for such a realisation,
one need not disregard
religious scriptures,
other literature,
traditions,
beliefs,
the sayings of the wise.
Yet none of these
need be followed blindly.
To understand the reality of life
one has to experience
the Truth himself.
Only such an experience
can transform one in real terms.

Such a transformation can happen,
and great strides can be made,
in the spheres of
peace and progress,
when you, as an individual,
and also as a race,
surrender yourself
before Mother Nature—
the manifest form
of Cosmic Energy
and, hence,
the source of all life—
completely,
comprehensively,
unconditionally,
without any hidden desire for
any reward.

When you surrender to Nature
in such a manner,
you start seeing
things from a broader perspective.
Tunnel vision gives way
to a universal outlook
and you realise
that you are
an important participant
in a multifaceted
and multilayered continuity—
a continuity of space,
of unending waves of energy,
of never-ending matter,
of time,
of past, present and future,
of organic and inorganic entities,
of actions and their results,

of emotions,
of ever-happening events,
of systems
otherwise so impeccable
yet dependent on each other
for sustenance.
A continuity
so incomprehensively vast,
and still growing,
at a scorching pace.
A continuity whose form
is ever in flux
but whose substance
never changes.
A continuity which,
by its very definition,
admits no separateness,
even though each of its particles

may have a distinct
and unique identity.
Each particle of this continuity,
of Nature,
is always in motion.
This continuity, in essence,
is a continuity of change.

Accordingly, you understand
you are an integral,
inseparable,
ever-evolving,
yet distinct,
and distinguishable part
of this most dynamic
yet perfectly stable,
all-pervading,
all-inclusive,

indivisible,
continuity,
namely, all creation.

The creator of this highly intricate
network of multiple continuity,
the universe,
we call 'Mother Nature'.
Whatever name you choose—
Creator,
Divine Will,
Supreme Power,
God,
or anything else—
it is the Ultimate Reality,
the Eternal Truth.

While surrendering before the Lord
you also come to realise
that though free
the Supreme Power
is bound by laws
created by Herself.

Whether you perceive Him
to be formless or in form
revealed by someone or self-evident,
is not relevant.
What is important is
your equation with Him,
your faith in Him,
and the quality of your surrender.
If you consider Him
to have a form,
some particular shape

and some specific qualities,
then believe
in that and only that form.
But your firm belief
in any one form
should not lead
you to disrespect
any other form,
or the concept of formlessness.
While surrendering to the Lord
you also realise
there can be no force
in matters of faith.
May you ever remain
firm in your belief
and yet
flexible in your approach.

In such a state of mind,
you remain
sensitive to criticism,
open to suggestion,
and prepared for course-correction.
While accommodating all points of view,
you remain firm in your belief,
and focused on your goal.

What matters is not the tone and tenor
but the feeling
in your surrender.
In the state of complete surrender,
you start living in Him
and eating out of His hand.
When your mind
remains filled

with contemplation
of the Lord,
no unwarranted thought
can trouble you for long.

Do not let your faith in God
depend on an event
which might
or might not have happened
in your day-to-day life.
Instead, know your faith
to be the very foundation
upon which the entire edifice
of your life
has been built.

God is vital
for, independent of Him,
you can have no existence.
In the same manner,
you are important to Him,
for no Whole can ever be complete
without its individual parts.

When you surrender to God
unconditionally,
the apparent dichotomy
of unchanging substance
and ever-changing form,
resolves itself
in your mind.
Since you come to know yourself
to be one with the Reality,

the Truth,
in its absolute form,
relative truth
starts revealing itself to you.
You start realising that
Truth for everyone
is the same;
yet differences in perceptions
will always remain.

Instead of computing
possible or probable
profits and losses
of surrender to the Lord,
you start rejoicing in the
very act of surrender.
Surrender may or may not

guarantee
every moment's ecstasy,
but it can ensure
that despondency, if any,
will be overcome.

What you are known as
is determined by the
perception of others
about you;
what you think
of yourself
determines your own reality.

When you want to meditate
upon Him,
do not start with
any preconceived notions.
Relax, let your thoughts fly,
wherever they want to go.
Do not fight them,
do not suppress them,
only be aware of them.
Slowly all thoughts
will begin
to calm down
and you will
start seeing Reality
as it is,
and not as you have been told
to believe.

Surrender to Him
not out of fear
or to get rid of any
feelings of guilt;
neither to seek any material gain
nor in the expectation of
divine intervention.
You surrender
for the sake
of surrender.
You surrender
not in the hope
of acquiring
supernatural powers
or for miraculous experiences,
but to seek knowledge—
about yourself,
your Creator,

your surroundings.
And to be aware
of your own self
and the purpose
of your life.

While surrendering before God
you do not seek from Him
wealth,
respectability,
or even bliss.
You earn wealth
through hard work,
you command respect
through your behaviour
and you realise
by experience

that your basic nature
is bliss
and bliss alone.
But you never forget
that it is He
who has made
it all possible.

When you surrender to God,
your creator,
provider,
teacher,
emancipator,
comprehensively
and without quid pro quo,
the whole of your life
becomes worship,

and any action, a prayer.
You start feeling
His presence,
His power,
His protection,
all the time
and everywhere.
Whether you take,
a baby step or a giant one,
it leads you
to Him.
You start merging
with Him,
slowly but surely.

In such a state of mind
you are neither
burdened with memories of the past,
nor fears of the future.
You are comfortable with
whatever you are,
wherever you are.

Surrender to God,
but never to fate.
A fatalist
is worse than a terrorist,
for while a terrorist kills others
a fatalist kills
his own willpower.

Complete surrender
is a state of merger
with the Lord.
In this state
you are aware
of your rights,
without being oblivious
to your duties.
Depending upon circumstances
and keeping in mind
the larger good,
you might forego
some of your rights,
but non-performance
of any duty
can never be an option.
You can surrender your rewards,
but never the actions.

Surrender can never be
an excuse for inaction,
because inaction is
the very antithesis
of evolution,
growth,
development.
And merger is
the antithesis
of escapism.

In the state of merger
you accept with gratitude
whatever comes your way;
but never negate the possibility
of greater effort
and better results.

Pray to the Lord
not for materialistic gains
or for creating
favourable situations.
Pray to Him
for the blessing of
capability
with which you can acquire
such gains
and also create
desirable situations
on your own.
Also pray
for the humility
with which you can accept
success,
and for grace
with which you can accept
failure.

Surrender to God,
but not to any godman,
for he who is incomplete himself,
cannot grant you completeness.

Merger with God
is not a magic wand,
which would solve instantly
all your problems.
It is, instead,
a process
of gaining knowledge
and understanding
at the intellectual level
and realising experientially
the ultimate Truth of life.
With realisation

you gain wisdom and strength
to face all situations fearlessly.
The state of merger
is the state
of realisation of Truth,
for in that state
of consciousness,
the only difference
between you and Him
is a difference in scale.

In the state of merger,
you have attained
nothing less than
the Lord Himself.
You are struggling as well,
for you have to always

keep pace
with the One,
one of whose important features
is dynamism.

Revel in the act of
surrender,
but do not get intoxicated
by the experience.
Let the theme of your life
change from
'I want'
to
'I rejoice'
and
'I am grateful'.

Surrender to the Lord,
is not some sudden,
one-time affair
or limited to the activity
of renunciation.
It can also not be depicted through
an ostensible show
of devotion.
It is a change of attitude,
a continuous thought-process,
which entails
a movement towards unity,
and away from divisiveness.
Towards oneness
and away from separation.

Merger with the Lord
results in
an
all-inclusive,
harmonious,
proactive,
manner of living.
In the state of merger
there is no separation,
and hence,
no stresses and strains.

You begin to merge
with the Lord
when you start feeling
His presence
all around.
You also understand

and try to perform better
your role
in His vibrant presence.

In the state of merger
you do not challenge,
or levy conditions,
or bargain
with the Lord.
The relationship
that has been established
between Him and you
becomes that of
a loving parent and child,
a caring teacher and student,
two friends.

If you want to attain oneness
with the Absolute
do not wait
for some miracle to happen,
do not wait for
some realised being to
come and save your soul;
do not let yourself be buried
under the debris of
unrealistic expectations.
Do not wait
for an auspicious occasion
but start right now.

Start thinking of
His omnipresence,
His perfection,

His impartiality;
and also start thanking Him
for making you
a part of such
a challenging yet delightful
experience, called 'life'.
Thank Him for
what He has made you
and also for what He has not;
thank Him for
whatever He has provided you with
and also for what He has not.

In the state of merger
you realise that
life is not a burden
to be carried

but a festival
to be celebrated.
Everyone has a unique role to play
in this carnival.

No one is ever completely successful
or a total failure.
Some may have more wealth,
while others may have better health.
Some may be socially recognised,
while others may be
intellectually acclaimed.
And so on.
Deficiency in one aspect
may be compensated
by Nature
in some other aspect.

An understanding
of this truth
leaves no scope for
inferiority or superiority complexes.
One is satisfied with
what one gets
without comparing
one's own failures with
the perceived successes
of others.

Only those
who consider
themselves to be failures
constantly try to find fault
with others.
This is their way of

equalisation.
In the state of merger
you know
no one is
a complete failure
no one is
a complete success.
You appreciate everyone appropriately
and do not find unnecessary fault
with anyone,
including your own self.

An egoist sees the world
through the prism of his arrogance.
He cuts himself off
from the realities of life,
and creates his own

world of make-believe.
He has his own standards
and scales
to measure everything.
Only those who massage
his bloated ego
are considered worthy
of any admiration.
Everyone else is held
to be condemnable.
In the state of merger,
you realise that
any view which is
disagreeable to you
need not necessarily be
wrong, unjust, or wicked.
Thus you try
to understand

the point of view of others,
and in the process
enable yourself to see
your own image
in their eyes.
And thus minimise
the distance
between you and them.
A feeling of oneness
and an urge for fair treatment
of everyone
is a natural corollary.

In such a state
of awakening
you also realise
that if an inflated ego

is an open invitation
to imminent destruction,
complete annihilation of ego
is equally damaging.
An egoless person is
condemned to lead a
vegetative life.
Only an aware ego,
which results in
a realistic assessment
of yourself
can protect you
against alienation
and ensure assimilation
with the different elements
and systems of Mother Nature.
Only a true picture
of one's potential

and inherent limitations
can create a suitable condition
for comprehensive growth.

In the state of merger,
you become
so expanded that
everyone is your own.
The more you attach yourself
emotionally to people around you,
the greater is the connection
between you and Nature.
The equation of your life
changes
from 'you versus others',
to 'you with others'.
You give to others

whatever you can,
you take from others
whatever you need,
but you are dependent
upon none.

In such a state of being
you threaten no one
and you are afraid of none.
You do not treat anyone unfairly
and also do not suffer
injustice from anyone.
Thus, the very matrix
of your relationship
with others
is transformed.
Detached analysis

of any relationship
enables you to see through
unrealistic expectations,
that you might have,
and also the genuine interest
and inherent limitations
of the other person.
You therefore prefer
to become
a supportive friend
instead of
a nagging partner.

Even while competing fiercely,
for survival
and for growth,
cooperation becomes the

basic theme of your life.
You can, in this manner,
defeat the ever-persistent feeling
of loneliness.
You can be alone
for any amount of time,
but never lonely.

You also realise that
on your own
you are nothing,
but as part of
an immense network
called life
you are yourself
a powerhouse of energy.
Though functional

only as part of the network,
you cannot afford
to loose your own identity.
It is your duty to protect
your distinctiveness,
for you have been made unique,
in every sense of the term,
by the Creator.
Your uniqueness
makes your life
worth living
and the phenomenon of life
interesting.

In the state of merger,
you consider Him alone
to be the doer

and yourself as only
an instrument through which
an action is performed.
All actions
are credited to Him
and all results
are accepted
with a sense
of gratitude.

At times
it becomes difficult
for you to decide
what is right,
what is wrong;
what is good for you
and what is not.

In such circumstances,
leave everything to Him.
He will make you do
whatever is correct,
and whatever He has
made you to do
will be in your
best interest.

In the process of merging
with Reality,
your ego, your self-image,
starts perceiving itself correctly.
You can then
never be arrogant,
for you consider
nothing as your own.

You also can
never suffer from
a lack of confidence;
for He, with all his resources,
is always with you.
You can do,
whatever you want,
for your own improvement,
for the betterment
of society,
and for the service
of mankind as a whole,
because in such a state of being,
you are freed
from the fear of failure,
and also from
the curse of self-condemnation.

One often passes through
phases of
confusion and uncertainty,
which generally arise
out of a multiplicity of choice.
Due to the availability of
equally viable options,
it may become difficult
to make a definite decision.
Doubts arise
even about decisions
already made.
In the state of merger
you realise
that in absolute terms,
nothing is right
and nothing is wrong.
You take decisions

and perform actions
as per the situations
you are placed in,
and using the wisdom
gained from
your past experiences.
And knowing that results
do not depend
entirely on your actions.
Numerous unknown forces
are at play,
hence results,
even if
they seem undesirable,
do not trouble you excessively.
There is not much scope
for repentance or doubt,
or confusion.

Thus you overcome
all sources of stress,
and all sources of strain.

In the process of merger
you understand
that if you are nice
you are nice to your own self;
and if your behaviour is obnoxious,
it is so for your own self.
For others are affected
by your behaviour
only marginally,
for a limited period,
whereas its effect on you
is comprehensive and
long-lasting.

In the state of merger,
your ego is as little removed
from the realities of life
as is possible.
You start seeing
things objectively.
As a result,
the distance between
you and Him
vanishes.

Creation being
the manifested form
of Cosmic Energy,
retains its essential qualities.
Mother Nature, thus,
continues to radiate
strength,
vibrancy,
harmony.
Despite superficial aberrations,
you always know
yourself
to be bliss
and bliss alone.
In such a state of realisation,
you tend to transcend
all limitations
imposed by time,

space,
and the sense organs.
Your self-esteem is
enhanced manifold
on the realisation that
you represent
a unique facet
of Him
at any particular time,
and space.

All your weaknesses
are exposed before you,
and all your strengths too
are revealed.
You get an opportunity
to erase your weaknesses,

and work on your strengths.
You also get an opportunity
to lighten your burden of
irrational beliefs,
unnecessary prejudices,
and unanswered questions,
which, otherwise,
you carry all the time.

In the state of merger,
being nearer to the Truth,
you can see both
the positive and negative aspects
of any situation.
But you highlight
and build upon
mainly,

rather, only,
the positive.
You have not only the
satisfaction of making
the right decision
but can also
rejoice in the fact
that you were able
to make an aware choice,
instead of
a mechanical decision.

In the state of merger,
you life becomes balanced.
You do not deny yourself
ordinary pleasures,
while avoiding

excessive indulgence.
You are not afraid
of imaginary pains,
while facing boldly
the real ones.
You take situations,
as they come,
and use them
to the best of your capability,
for your own benefit
and that of others.

When you surrender to the Lord,
you surrender
not to an
abstract idea,
but to the laws framed

and the systems established
by Him.
You work in conformity
with them.
You are at peace with yourself
and your surroundings.
Your individual will
merges with Divine Will.
And you put yourself,
in control of your life,
but without ever forgetting
that the ultimate control
is always
in His hands.

Surrendering before the Lord
and taking charge
of one's life
are not contradictory.
Rather, they mean the same thing.
For, when you merge
with Him,
you start acquiring
His traits
resultantly emerging stronger.
Surrender does not
diminish your capacity
to achieve desired results.
Instead, it is enhanced
through the unleashing of
dormant energy within you.
As a result,
you can transform yourself,

improve your surroundings,
impact society as a whole.
Thus, you live an aware life,
not a mechanical one.

The satisfaction bestowed upon you
by the Lord
is not an inert emotion,
but an aware satisfaction.
Even when you are
fully satisfied with
whatever you have attained,
the urge for growth
and contributing
to others' welfare
not only remains,
but increases exponentially.

At the same time
condemnation of oneself
and criticism of others
becomes reduced substantially.

In the state of merger,
you also come to realise
that man by his very constitution
is imperfect.
You thus accept yourself
with all your infirmities,
and also others
with all their shortcomings.
Aware that
you and everyone else
are part of a ceaseless continuity,
you never judge your own

or anyone else's behaviour
in isolation.
Even if an action
appears ridiculous,
as part of a continuity
of action and reaction,
it is possible that it might
make perfect sense.
Because you can
place various behavioural patterns
in proper perspective,
instead of being judgmental,
you become
increasingly empathetic.

One of the traits
unique to mankind
is hypocrisy.
One wants to project oneself
to be what one knows one is not,
and deny
what one knows
for sure one is.
There is a gap
between one's real self
and its depiction.
In the state of merger
you know the futility
of presenting a picture
you know to be false.
Instead, you try to lessen
the gap between
reality and its projection,

by achieving more
and bragging less.
And so you live
a simple and successful life.

Though the path to merger may be
long,
uneven,
and sometimes even slippery,
the experience of walking it
is certainly
its own reward.

In such a state of realisation,
you may or may not get
what you want;
but you would certainly
be happy
with whatever you get.

In the state of merger
you realise
that everyone is assured
a constant supply of energy,
life force,
from that incessant source
of energy—
the Supreme Lord.
The quantities may vary
depending upon the capabilities

of your body and mind,
and also your willpower,
but an uninterrupted supply
of energy is assured
till your last breath.

You also come to know
that energy is
neither positive
nor negative.
Energy is energy,
the medium through which
organic and inorganic entities
perform various actions.
Good deeds produce good vibes
and the accompanying energy
is perceived as good.

How you manage
and utilise
this energy
for your own benefit,
and for the benefit
of everyone else,
is what the art of living
is all about.

You live life at
three distinct
but inseparable
and interdependent
levels of existence.
The levels—
the physical,
the mental and
the conscious—

correspond to what,
in common parlance,
is known as
the body, mind and soul.
These levels of being
supplement and complement
each other,
and, thus, constitute
an organic whole.
No mind,
no body,
nor the mind-body complex
can survive
in isolation.
Consciousness is the force behind
thought, action,
movement.

Whereas your behaviour
at the physical level
is determined by instinct,
at the mental level
it is influenced
by reason on the one hand,
and impulse on the other.
It is only at
the conscious level
that you realise
yourself to be
essentially bliss,
pure consciousness energy,
that is surrounded
from time to time
by configurations of other forms
of energy and matter
and their attendant emotions.

At the physical level,
your behaviour is primarily determined
by the instinct
towards self-preservation.
At the psychological level,
you are tormented constantly
by the devils of fear, guilt,
and their numerous variants.
It is only at the level
of consciousness
that you are guided
by those invaluable gifts
from the Lord;
of love,
compassion,
kindness.

Surrender before the Lord,
can be comprehensive and meaningful,
only if there is a simultaneous merger
at all the three levels
of existence.

Surrendering to the Lord
at the physical level
implies living naturally—
relying on
natural ways of production,
consumption and disposal,
and being less dependent upon
artificial means.
When you follow gladly
the principles of Nature,
and work in consonance with

her various systems
evolved over millennia,
the equilibrium between
the different elements of Nature
is strengthened.
Thus, the merger
of the individual
with Cosmic Reality
at the physical level
leads to
natural, healthy living.

The merger of the individual mind
with the Cosmic Mind
is more challenging.
Because the subconscious mind,
which is a major determining factor

in human behaviour
is a storehouse of
unfounded doubts,
absurd ideas and
ridiculous plans.
Such junk often gets accumulated
on account of
the unpleasant outcomes
of various experiences
one goes through in life.
In the state of merger,
the truth about the real traits
of the mind becomes clear,
and its complexities
begin to reveal themselves.
You become more conscious
of your thoughts
and as a result

the superfluous garbage
collected over the years
in the subconscious mind
clears up and
your dependence
upon the subconscious—
the unorganised and the irrational part
of the mind—
begins to decrease.
Such a cleaning procedure
leads to rational thinking.

In such a state of awakening
you find that
one of the basic ingredients
of the mind
is dissatisfaction.

The human mind,
and thus a human being,
cannot remain satisfied
for long.
Dissatisfaction appears,
from time to time,
in its myriad complex forms.
To overcome this,
one's mind tries
not only to influence
and control others,
but also to belittle them.
Desires continue to arise
in the mind,
one after the other.
Fulfillment of all desires
is never possible,
for the fulfillment

of one desire
automatically leads to
the rise of
another, bigger one.
Non-fulfillment
of all desires
results in further dissatisfaction
and distress.
One, is thus caught, in a vicious circle.
Desire, being integral to human nature,
cannot be shooed away,
shied away from;
or suppressed.
But it can certainly be harnessed
for harmonious growth
and joyful living.
Thus, desire need not be
denied or decried.

Let your desire flourish
for desire is the dynamo of life.
Surrender before the Lord
does not mean
a death of dreams,
a fading away of hopes,
a slackness in action.
Surrender before the Lord
bestows one with
the understanding
that all desires cannot be fulfilled,
all dreams need not be realised,
all hopes cannot be met,
and results of actions,
though inherent in that action,
need not necessarily be as
per your expectations.
Thus, while toiling

in pursuit of your targets,
for the fructification of
your desires, dreams and hopes,
you are spared
the tyranny of
unreasonable expectations.

In the state of realisation
you also ensure
that desire
does not degenerate
into lust
and you do not
fall prey
to over-indulgence.

Let ambition accelerate
the speed of your life,
but never switch off
the governor of wisdom,
for it can save you
from many unforeseen collisions.
Only an unconditional surrender
before the Lord
can equip you with
the wonderful instrument
of this wisdom.

In such a state of mind,
even when involved
fully in your work,
you have no time
or inclination

to lament the non-realisation
of desired results.
In this manner,
you can grow
without suffering
the pangs
of distress
and dissatisfaction.

In an awakened state
you are not afraid
of your shortcomings
being exposed.
You do not waste
your energy
in covering up
your infirmities.

Instead, you get to their root
and try either to eliminate them
or admit to them openly.

When you surrender to Him
you leave everything to the Lord;
to His judgment,
His benevolence,
His grace.
You are relieved
of all fears, guilt,
pride and prejudices.
You realise that
whereas superstitions are
direct manifestations of fear,
obscure beliefs,
irrational dogmas,

meaningless rituals,
are camouflages devised
to obviate various fears.
As you overcome
deep-rooted fears
through awareness,
for you,
these means of
mass exploitation
mean nothing.
And you can manage
your psychological affairs
with courage and determination.

You hand over
all your worries
to Him

and, in return,
you get hope.
Restlessness gives way
to serenity
generated from understanding,
pregnant with hope,
filled with confidence.

When you merge with the Lord
at the level of consciousness,
your consciousness merges
with Universal Consciousness.
You come to know yourself
as an integral and
inseparable part of
pure energy,
the essential nature of which

is bliss.
You come to know
of bliss
not only at the intellectual level,
but also at the experiential level.
You realise yourself to be
nothing but bliss—
bliss that means
incessant love for the Lord,
ever-increasing joy,
benevolent strength,
universal compassion,
dynamic peace,
and whatever else you long for.
You realise the Truth—
the fundamental realities
of existence.
At the intellectual level,

you understand better
what is true,
what is false.
At the level of the sense-organs,
you are closer to the truth.
At all levels of existence,
you are blessed with
a life of truthfulness.

In such a state of being,
the truth about
your own behaviour
will dawn upon you.
You begin to understand
that most interpersonal problems
arise not only because
you have inflated your ego,

but also because you have
demonised others
in your mind.
Your behaviour is often guided
by apprehensions
you carry about others.
You want to vanquish the monster
before it devours you,
and in the process
you provide enough reason
to others
to be apprehensive
about you.
In the state of merger
you realise that
such demonisation,
most of the times,
is a product
of your imagination only.

The others
may be as nice as you are,
or what you
want them to be.

In the state of merger,
bliss remains the
underlying theme
of your life.
Even while performing
any difficult act,
or facing an adverse situation,
the predominant thought
in your mind
remains the thought
of blissfulness.

Understanding life
at all the three levels
of existence
is real empowerment,
of the body,
the mind,
and the soul.

In such a state of realisation
you understand
that you are
primarily bliss,
and as a result
often experience ecstasy.
You also understand that
on its own
such an ecstasy
is like a flower

beautiful and fragrant,
but grown on
a desolate piece of land.
You understand
that the experience
of any joy
is meaningless
if not shared.
You not only wish to share
your happiness with others,
you also let them share
their pain with you.
You begin to respect
their sentiments
and also try to become
a part of their dreams.

The state of merger,
being the state of enlightenment,
makes you understand
that action and inaction,
success and failure,
comfort and discomfort,
pleasure and pain,
and other such conditions,
are functions of body and mind
and relate to the outer world.
But bliss
being the function of consciousness
relates almost exclusively
to your inner world.

The state of merger
can enable you to relish
the melodious music
of the deep silence within,
even while responding appropriately
to the multiple cacophonies
of the outer world.

In such a state of being,
you neither seek instant gratification
in material things,
nor do you seek
the elusive blessedness
in escape to a
make-believe inner world.
Instead, you discover
your basic nature

to be bliss,
and bliss alone,
through your own experience.

The inner bliss and
the outer trappings
are not contradictory.
These, in fact,
complement and supplement
each other.

In a state of realisation,
you also come to understand
that any amount of inner peace
without reasonable achievements
to your credit

in the outer world
is nameless,
and any achievement
in the outer world
without inner peace
is meaningless.
Only a co-ordinated growth
in both spheres of life,
on all the three levels
of existence,
can make it
truly purposeful
and a rewarding experience.

In such a state
of comprehensive growth
you understand

that you can establish
your relevance
in the forest of life
only when your roots are deep,
your trunk strong,
branches widespread,
flowers beautiful and fragrant,
and also when your fruits
are tasty and beneficial.
In such a state of realisation,
you learn to be
healthy at the physical level,
happy at the psychological level,
and you strive to establish harmony
at the consciousness level.

Accordingly you begin to live
in awareness.
Whereas earlier
involuntary thoughts
would keep arising
in your mind,
in the aware state
you can let a thought in,
or deny it the privilege
of entering your mind-space.
Whereas earlier
an act was performed by you
under the force of circumstances,
now you not only decide
to do or not do something,
but also decide the manner
in which you will do it.
At the same time,

you remain prepared
to face the consequences
of your actions.

So, while experiencing gladly
the tumult, turmoil and turbulence
arising from
decisions taken and actions performed,
you remain intensely aware
of your essential nature,
and accordingly enjoy
the ecstasy of
your own being,
and also of everyone else.

Becoming aware
of your essential nature,
realising the fact that
you are
an incarnation of bliss,
does not lead you
to become arrogant,
because you consider
everyone else too
to have been
similarly blessed.
Thus, you reach
the top of the world,
without trampling
on anyone else.

In such a state of being
you remain proud
of your own self,
your surroundings,
your relationships,
your temporal achievements,
and the divine blessings
bestowed upon you.
But you never
become arrogant
about anything.

When you merge with the Lord
at all three levels of existence,
you realise that you are
a centre of conscious energy,
surrounded simultaneously

by mental and physical energy.
When you identify
with consciousness
as your real self,
you are bound less
by the limitations
of the body
and the machinations
of the mind.

You also realise
no level of existence
is unimportant.
If consciousness is
the very essence of life,
the mind-body complex
is the only instrument

through which it can express itself.
Thus, without belittling
your psychosomatic
needs, aspirations, pleasures, pains,
and without evading your responsibilities,
you identify yourself increasingly
with consciousness
and so experience
incessant bliss.

In the state of realisation
you do not treat creation
as illusion,
for it is the only world
you know for sure.
Everything else is
in the realm of speculation.

You also do not undermine
the importance of consciousness
for it is the only medium
through which you create
your own self-image
and also relate
to the outside world.

In such a state
of awareness,
instead of being allured by
the expectation of a big catch
sometime in future,
you begin to rejoice in
whatever is happening
from moment to moment.

Such an attitude,
instead of hindering,
in fact promotes
future accomplishments.

By giving every level of existence
importance due to it,
you live a balanced life.
An achievement in one sphere of life
may afford you
name and fame,
for some time,
but can never guarantee
a life of perpetual satisfaction.
When you merge with the Lord,
at all the three levels of existence

without any reservations,
you achieve holistic growth.
A balanced life
is individually satisfying
and socially relevant.
It helps maintain
the subtle cosmic equilibrium,
and helps realise
the real purpose of existence—
a blissful, harmonious, and interesting life.
Merger with the Lord
makes it possible
for you to lead
with effortless ease
such a wondrous life,
and achieve
the larger goal of life.

On the path to realisation
you come to understand
what spirituality is,
and who can be called
a spiritual person.
You don't call anyone 'spiritual'
only because he claims to possess
mysterious powers,
or dresses up in
a particular fashion.
You are spiritual
only when you have established
a comfortable relationship
with the Creator,
and have understood the
ultimate purpose of life.
You then become a facilitator
in the realisation of this purpose.

Even though bliss and harmony
are essential ingredients
of human life,
challenges are also inherent
in any situation.
For only a challenging life
can be an interesting life.
Apart from the challenges
presented by Nature herself,
many challenges arise
from interpersonal relationships.
At any point in your life,
you have numerous relationships.
Your identity could also be
determined by the relationships
you are born into,
or have established
over a period of time,

with various individual
and collective entities.
Relationships give rise
to myriad emotions.
In the state of merger,
being aware of the source
of all emotions,
you enjoy them
without being overwhelmed.

Emotions are integral to one's life,
and an emotionless life
would certainly be
uninteresting and colourless.
Some emotions
such as
love, affection, kindness,

piety and co-operation,
are ingrained in your system.
Such emotions make life meaningful.
Life is full
of irritants that arise
from past memories,
present problems,
and future uncertainties.
You might have been
subjected to ridicule
or criticised,
and made to face
allegations and accusations.
You might also be nursing
some sorrows or grudges.
Due to all this,
you burn in the fires
of jealousy,

suffer recurring bouts of anger,
are tormented by the urge for revenge.
At times you are tempted
by the apparent beauty
of the gardens of greed,
but these often prove
to be illusory,
even slippery.
You may experience
feelings of
helplessness and frustration
because of
perceived or real
psychosomatic situations.
Howsoever hard you may try
you cannot wish away
these feelings of despondency.

In the state of realisation,
you come to understand
that all types of emotions
exist in this world.
You attract these
at a particular time
according to your nature,
behaviour and actions
at that point of time.

Merger does not lead
to the fading out
of emotions.
Rather, it makes you realise
that some of these emotions
are part of your real nature
and can enrich

your life immensely.
Other emotions,
acquired due to
unpleasant experiences,
only serve to make
your life miserable.
Even though the state of merger
cannot guarantee the absence
of situations that cause
sadness and depression,
it does make you aware
of the source
of all your negative emotions.
Since you realise
your essential nature to be
bliss and bliss alone,
you also understand
that feelings of dissatisfaction

are superficial and transitory.
Thus the clouds
of despondency,
automatically wither away.
You can, in this manner,
manage your emotions,
and yourself,
much more effectively.

In the state of realisation,
you also understand
that while negative traits
are acquired through
different experiences of life,
bliss is one's essential nature.
The traits that have been learnt
can be unlearned as well,

but one's essential nature
can never be changed.
Under no circumstances
can you let
these minor irritants
overshadow the essential
beauty of life
and overwhelm your true nature
of bliss.

In such a state of being
you not only realise
yourself to be bliss
and bliss alone,
you are also ready
to share the message
of incessant joy

with anyone
who is willing
to listen.

Reality being
so dynamic, rhythmic
and focused
on the ultimate purpose of life,
in the process of merger
you also begin to
acquire these qualities.
Keeping in mind,
the ultimate purpose,
you fix for yourself
different aims and goals,
at different times.
Whatever the situation,
you are never oblivious
to your ultimate purpose,

and, so, the aims and goals
you choose
remain in consonance
with the larger, common good.

Non-realisation of any goal
does not
perturb you excessively,
because it does not affect
the ultimate purpose of life.
Non-realisation of any goal
does not make you stubborn
about achieving it,
for in the light of awareness,
you can see much bigger
and better alternatives.

Achievement in various fields
is one of the
most important parameters
of success in life.
But in the state of merger,
one realises that success at any cost,
cannot be one's life's purpose.
Success is important,
but more important
is the manner in which
it is achieved,
and still more important
is how one receives it,
deals with it,
and digests it.

Moderate success
without compromising
with one's physical health,
psychic wellness,
family ties,
and social responsibilities,
is much better than
a meteoric rise
achieved at the cost of
one's conscience.
Only success well-earned
and well-managed
can ensure
long-lasting satisfaction
for your own self
and for everybody else.

In the state of awakening
you also understand
that success is meaningless
unless you acquire
the art of accepting, absorbing,
and drawing appropriate lessons
from your failures.

In such a state of merger
you realise that
you are not necessarily the
wisest, most intelligent person
on this earth.
You, thus, learn to respect
others' point of view.
You also realise
that no heavenly duty

has been cast upon you
to mould
the rest of the world
in the cast you think to be right.
You do sincerely what you
think is correct.
Others can, if they want,
follow your example.
You can, hence, be spared
much self-created responsibility
and frustration.

If your surrender before the Lord
does not make you
a better person,
more pleasant,
more open to criticism,
and generally more helpful,
and it does not help you
learn more,
become meaningfully creative,
and does not bestow upon you
a habit of sharing,
then your surrender
is either insincere
or incomplete.
If your so-called surrender
makes you colourless,
devoid of genuine emotions,

interested only in the after-life,
then the merger, if any,
is certainly misdirected.

Comprehensive merger with the Lord,
makes you see the larger picture,
and so helps you embody
a strong value system,
peaceful co-existence,
and universal happiness.

You accept yourself
as you are,
whatever you are,
wherever you are.

Your acceptance and respect
for yourself
provides you a platform
to grow exponentially,
without being arrogant
or unduly stressed.

In the state of merger
you acquire a sense of fulfillment.
You know not what inadequacy is,
and you know not incompleteness.
You do realise
the true meaning
of the process of evolution—
you can survive only
if you keep growing.

Therefore your struggle
for growth
and further growth
must go on
forever.

In such a state of realisation
you also understand
that paths of
devotion,
knowledge,
action,
service,
which you think can lead you
to the Lord,
are not exclusive

and do not contradict,
compete, or come in conflict
with one another.
These, in fact,
complement and supplement
one another
and help to make you
complete.
You also understand that
these concepts
are not
shrouded in any mystery
and need not be studded
with the jugglery of words.
They only depict
the predominant attitude
you have towards life.

In the state of merger
you know the source of all existence
to be consciousness energy
which connotes
a vibrant peace,
harmonious dynamism,
an unending joy,
and other such qualities
which form the core of life.
Everything else
is only peripheral.
After this enlightenment,
you not only live
at the source,
but also strive
to shine in the same.

In such a state of awakening,
each day brings
a new sun,
fresh energy,
undiminishing vigour,
renewed determination.
And each night
a new moon,
refreshing calm,
deep relaxation,
an all-pervading serenity,
the hope for
a better tomorrow.

Thus, in the state of merger,
you live a life
full of confidence,
in communion with the Lord,

in conformity with His laws,
in consonance with society and Nature.
Since existence is
an eternal,
dynamic,
ever-evolving phenomenon,
merger of a part
with the whole
is a process
which can never be finished.
During this churning,
you also realise
that knowledge of any subject
is never complete,
and the process of learning
can never come
to
an end.